NOVEL
ASSISTANT
for kids!!!

Novel Assistant Publishing

Ireland

DEDICATION

*This novel assisting journal for kids around the globe is fondly dedicated to
Laurel and Riley,*

the most charming characters of my life story.

CONTENTS

NOVEL ASSISTANT FOR KIDS!!!

We at Novel Assistant Publishing think that KIDS ROCK!!

We also think that if there is anyone in the entire world that has the creativity and imagination to create a story...it is YOU!!!

You can WRITE a BOOK!!!

Think about what story you want to tell. Which characters will play out your story? They will need names, of course, but even more than that!!

First, write the title of your book on the next page. Write your name as the author!! (You, of course, can use a pen name!) Write the genre of your novel. (E.g. sci-fi, comedy, or fantasy)

Bring your characters to life by asking them questions in your *Character Development* section. Get to know each of your characters by "taking a walk around in their shoes."

Then...

Plan out your story line in the *My Novel* section of your book! Do some free writing, fill up your timelines, and then plot out each chapter so that you are ready to write!

When you have finished writing your novel, check the next to last page for tips and ideas of what to do with your novel and where you can share it!

We hope this novel planner is helpful to guide you through planning and writing your very own novel!

Best of Luck, writer!

-Novel Assistant Publishing

TITLE PAGE

(Book Title)

(Author)

(Genre)

STORY SUMMARY

STORY SUMMARY

CHARACTER DEVELOPMENT

Your novel needs characters. They can be people, animals, aliens, magical creatures, or whatever you can imagine! They will play out a story for the readers. One very important step that authors take to make their novels outstanding is developing their characters.

A good way to develop your characters is to first name them! Give your characters memorable names by really thinking about what name would set them apart from other characters. There are so many names used throughout history. You could combine names and even create new names that have never been used before!

Once you have given your character a name, take them to a character interview! For example, the character you named as number one should be your "protagonist", also known as your main character. Write their name in the "character one" page, and then imagine that they are sitting in front of you as you ask them each interview question. Use your amazing imagination and write down what you think they would answer! After you interview each character, turn things around in the author's notes section. YOU…are the author of your novel! Ask yourself about each character and really get to know who they are.

Developing Characters as though they are real, will make the difference in your writing! Do not ever skip this step… the best writers in the world have taken the time to fully develop their characters! Now, it is your turn! We can't wait to see what interesting characters you come up with! Best of luck author…X

Get Creative!!...Draw or paste pictures relating to your novel:

CHARACTER LIST

Name your characters, here:

1. addie marth

2. kelli marth

3. annie glick

4. will glick

5. Daneille daring

6. Sheirff donskey

7. Julie walken

8.

9.

10.

Now, take each character and interview them in the next section:

CHARACTER ONE

1) What is your full name?

addie gianna marth

2) How old are you and what is your gender or species?

11\female

3) What colour is your hair; your eyes; your skin?

Brown\Brown\white

4) Describe your physical appearance:

meiedum\ skinny

5) Who are your friends?

ivy, Julie, and annie

6) Who is your best friend?

annie

7) What do you like to do in your spare time?

read

8) Who are your parents?

rida marth
landon marth

9) Who are your grandparents?

gianna marth
Bob marth

8

10) Where do you live?

glass   Street

11) Where do you go to school?

Washinton middle Sch-
ool

12) Do you play sports? If so, what sports do you like to play?

13) Do you enjoy music? If so, what type of music do you like?

country

14) What are your likes?

_?_

15) What are your dislikes?

ants.

16) Do you have any pets or are you a pet?

hamster

17) What makes you laugh?

witted   Jokes

9

18) What shocks or offends you?

talking behind back (dislike as well)

19) What do you care about?

family, friends e necklace of a family or promise

20) What is your biggest fear?

ants

21) Do you have any secrets?

22) Share a funny fact about yourself:

my real name was addison until my dad told me what Mb: are.

23) What is the best thing that has ever happened to you?

?

24) What is the worst thing that has ever happened to you?

?

25) What do you dream about?

falling alot,

AUTHOR NOTES ON THIS CHARACTER

Pretend you are alone with this character... who are they really?

Kind, passionate, foucesed.

What is special about them?

Determined to do a certin thing.

What is different about them?

Write 10 words about this character as if you have known them their whole life.

nice, passionate, foucesed, smiley neat, orginized, in the moment, Down to earth

Draw or paste a picture of your character here:

CHARACTER TWO

1) What is your full name?

Kelli Sarah marth

2) How old are you and what is your gender or species?

female

3) What colour is your hair; your eyes; your skin?

brown Brown white

4) Describe your physical appearance:

medum skinny

5) Who are your friends?

everyone at washington
middle school. and darville

6) Who is your best friend?

daneille

7) What do you like to do in your spare time?

bump up my status

8) Who are your parents?

Tida marth
landon marth

9) Who are your grandparents?

gianna marth
Bob marth

10) Where do you live?

glass st

11) Where do you go to school?

Washington middle school

12) Do you play sports? If so, what sports do you like to play?

soccer

13) Do you enjoy music? If so, what type of music do you like?

pop

14) What are your likes?

social media

15) What are your dislikes?

dad jokes

16) Do you have any pets or are you a pet?

hamster

17) What makes you laugh?

dad jokes (i can't help it)

13

18) What shocks or offends you?

people calling

_me s..._

19) What do you care about?

Obvi. family & friends

20) What is your biggest fear?

Baby Vida

21) Do you have any secrets?

_no_

22) Share a funny fact about yourself:

I was born

with a desise called "ti k

23) What is the best thing that has ever happened to you?

_?_

24) What is the worst thing that has ever happened to you?

_?_

25) What do you dream about?

random stuff

AUTHOR NOTES ON THIS CHARACTER

Pretend you are alone with this character... who are they really?

everything you can imagine or an it girl

What is special about them?

they have this snort-laugh

What is different about them?

Write 10 words about this character as if you have known them their whole life.

sassy silly kind smart-alked crazy

Draw or paste a picture of your character here:

CHARACTER THREE

1) What is your full name?

annie hannah glick

2) How old are you and what is your gender or species?

11 / female

3) What colour is your hair; your eyes; your skin?

Blonde, Blue, white

4) Describe your physical appearance:

5) Who are your friends?

6) Who is your best friend?

addie

7) What do you like to do in your spare time?

a iay

8) Who are your parents?

Stacy glick
Will glick

9) Who are your grandparents?

10) Where do you live?

_____

_____

11) Where do you go to school?

_____

_____

12) Do you play sports? If so, what sports do you like to play?

_____

_____

13) Do you enjoy music? If so, what type of music do you like?

_____

_____

14) What are your likes?

_____

_____

15) What are your dislikes?

_____

_____

_____

16) Do you have any pets or are you a pet?

_____

_____

17) What makes you laugh?

_____

_____

18) What shocks or offends you?

_____

_____

19) What do you care about?

_____

_____

20) What is your biggest fear?

_____

_____

21) Do you have any secrets?

_____

_____

22) Share a funny fact about yourself:

_____

_____

23) What is the best thing that has ever happened to you?

_____

_____

24) What is the worst thing that has ever happened to you?

_____

_____

25) What do you dream about?

_____

_____

AUTHOR NOTES ON THIS CHARACTER

Pretend you are alone with this character... who are they really?

_____

_____

What is special about them?

_____

_____

What is different about them?

_____

_____

Write 10 words about this character as if you have known them their whole life.

_____

_____

Draw or paste a picture of your character here:

CHARACTER FOUR

1) What is your full name?

_____

2) How old are you and what is your gender or species?

_____

3) What colour is your hair; your eyes; your skin?

_____

4) Describe your physical appearance:

_____

_____

5) Who are your friends?

_____

_____

6) Who is your best friend?

_____

7) What do you like to do in your spare time?

_____

_____

8) Who are your parents?

_____

_____

9) Who are your grandparents?

_____

_____

10) Where do you live?

_____

_____

11) Where do you go to school?

_____

_____

12) Do you play sports? If so, what sports do you like to play?

_____

_____

13) Do you enjoy music? If so, what type of music do you like?

_____

_____

14) What are your likes?

_____

_____

15) What are your dislikes?

_____

_____

_____

16) Do you have any pets or are you a pet?

_____

_____

17) What makes you laugh?

_____

_____

18) What shocks or offends you?

_____

_____

19) What do you care about?

_____

_____

20) What is your biggest fear?

_____

_____

21) Do you have any secrets?

_____

_____

22) Share a funny fact about yourself:

_____

_____

23) What is the best thing that has ever happened to you?

_____

_____

24) What is the worst thing that has ever happened to you?

_____

_____

25) What do you dream about?

_____

_____

AUTHOR NOTES ON THIS CHARACTER

Pretend you are alone with this character... who are they really?

_____

_____

What is special about them?

_____

_____

What is different about them?

_____

_____

Write 10 words about this character as if you have known them their whole life.

_____

_____

Draw or paste a picture of your character here:

CHARACTER FIVE

1) What is your full name?

_____

2) How old are you and what is your gender or species?

_____

3) What colour is your hair; your eyes; your skin?

_____

4) Describe your physical appearance:

_____

_____

5) Who are your friends?

_____

_____

6) Who is your best friend?

_____

7) What do you like to do in your spare time?

_____

_____

8) Who are your parents?

_____

_____

9) Who are your grandparents?

_____

_____

10) Where do you live?

_____

_____

11) Where do you go to school?

_____

_____

12) Do you play sports? If so, what sports do you like to play?

_____

_____

13) Do you enjoy music? If so, what type of music do you like?

_____

_____

14) What are your likes?

_____

_____

15) What are your dislikes?

_____

_____

_____

16) Do you have any pets or are you a pet?

_____

_____

17) What makes you laugh?

_____

_____

18) What shocks or offends you?

_____

_____

19) What do you care about?

_____

_____

20) What is your biggest fear?

_____

_____

21) Do you have any secrets?

_____

_____

22) Share a funny fact about yourself:

_____

_____

23) What is the best thing that has ever happened to you?

_____

_____

24) What is the worst thing that has ever happened to you?

_____

_____

25) What do you dream about?

_____

_____

AUTHOR NOTES ON THIS CHARACTER

Pretend you are alone with this character... who are they really?

_____

_____

What is special about them?

_____

_____

What is different about them?

_____

_____

Write 10 words about this character as if you have known them their whole life.

_____

_____

Draw or paste a picture of your character here:

CHARACTER SIX

1) What is your full name?

_____

2) How old are you and what is your gender or species?

_____

3) What colour is your hair; your eyes; your skin?

_____

4) Describe your physical appearance:

_____

_____

5) Who are your friends?

_____

_____

6) Who is your best friend?

_____

7) What do you like to do in your spare time?

_____

_____

8) Who are your parents?

_____

_____

9) Who are your grandparents?

_____

_____

10) Where do you live?

_____

_____

11) Where do you go to school?

_____

_____

12) Do you play sports? If so, what sports do you like to play?

_____

_____

13) Do you enjoy music? If so, what type of music do you like?

_____

_____

14) What are your likes?

_____

_____

15) What are your dislikes?

_____

_____

_____

16) Do you have any pets or are you a pet?

_____

_____

17) What makes you laugh?

_____

_____

18) What shocks or offends you?

_____

_____

19) What do you care about?

_____

_____

20) What is your biggest fear?

_____

_____

21) Do you have any secrets?

_____

_____

22) Share a funny fact about yourself:

_____

_____

23) What is the best thing that has ever happened to you?

_____

_____

24) What is the worst thing that has ever happened to you?

_____

_____

25) What do you dream about?

_____

_____

AUTHOR NOTES ON THIS CHARACTER

Pretend you are alone with this character... who are they really?

_____

_____

What is special about them?

_____

_____

What is different about them?

_____

_____

Write 10 words about this character as if you have known them their whole life.

_____

_____

Draw or paste a picture of your character here:

CHARACTER SEVEN

1) What is your full name?

_____

2) How old are you and what is your gender or species?

_____

3) What colour is your hair; your eyes; your skin?

_____

4) Describe your physical appearance:

_____

_____

5) Who are your friends?

_____

_____

6) Who is your best friend?

_____

7) What do you like to do in your spare time?

_____

_____

8) Who are your parents?

_____

_____

9) Who are your grandparents?

_____

_____

10) Where do you live?

_____

_____

11) Where do you go to school?

_____

_____

12) Do you play sports? If so, what sports do you like to play?

_____

_____

13) Do you enjoy music? If so, what type of music do you like?

_____

_____

14) What are your likes?

_____

_____

15) What are your dislikes?

_____

_____

_____

16) Do you have any pets or are you a pet?

_____

_____

17) What makes you laugh?

_____

_____

18) What shocks or offends you?

_____

_____

19) What do you care about?

_____

_____

20) What is your biggest fear?

_____

_____

21) Do you have any secrets?

_____

_____

22) Share a funny fact about yourself:

_____

_____

23) What is the best thing that has ever happened to you?

_____

_____

24) What is the worst thing that has ever happened to you?

_____

_____

25) What do you dream about?

_____

_____

AUTHOR NOTES ON THIS CHARACTER

Pretend you are alone with this character... who are they really?

_____

_____

What is special about them?

_____

_____

What is different about them?

_____

_____

Write 10 words about this character as if you have known them their whole life.

_____

_____

Draw or paste a picture of your character here:

CHARACTER EIGHT

1) What is your full name?

_____

2) How old are you and what is your gender or species?

_____

3) What colour is your hair; your eyes; your skin?

_____

4) Describe your physical appearance:

_____

_____

5) Who are your friends?

_____

_____

6) Who is your best friend?

_____

7) What do you like to do in your spare time?

_____

_____

8) Who are your parents?

_____

_____

9) Who are your grandparents?

_____

_____

10) Where do you live?

_____

_____

11) Where do you go to school?

_____

_____

12) Do you play sports? If so, what sports do you like to play?

_____

_____

13) Do you enjoy music? If so, what type of music do you like?

_____

_____

14) What are your likes?

_____

_____

15) What are your dislikes?

_____

_____

_____

16) Do you have any pets or are you a pet?

_____

_____

17) What makes you laugh?

_____

_____

18) What shocks or offends you?

_____

_____

19) What do you care about?

_____

_____

20) What is your biggest fear?

_____

_____

21) Do you have any secrets?

_____

_____

22) Share a funny fact about yourself:

_____

_____

23) What is the best thing that has ever happened to you?

_____

_____

24) What is the worst thing that has ever happened to you?

_____

_____

25) What do you dream about?

_____

_____

AUTHOR NOTES ON THIS CHARACTER

Pretend you are alone with this character... who are they really?

_____

_____

What is special about them?

_____

_____

What is different about them?

_____

_____

Write 10 words about this character as if you have known them their whole life.

_____

_____

Draw or paste a picture of your character here:

CHARACTER NINE

1) What is your full name?

_____

2) How old are you and what is your gender or species?

_____

3) What colour is your hair; your eyes; your skin?

_____

4) Describe your physical appearance:

_____

_____

5) Who are your friends?

_____

_____

6) Who is your best friend?

_____

7) What do you like to do in your spare time?

_____

_____

8) Who are your parents?

_____

_____

9) Who are your grandparents?

_____

_____

10) Where do you live?

_____

_____

11) Where do you go to school?

_____

_____

12) Do you play sports? If so, what sports do you like to play?

_____

_____

13) Do you enjoy music? If so, what type of music do you like?

_____

_____

14) What are your likes?

_____

_____

15) What are your dislikes?

_____

_____

_____

16) Do you have any pets or are you a pet?

_____

_____

17) What makes you laugh?

_____

_____

18) What shocks or offends you?

_____

_____

19) What do you care about?

_____

_____

20) What is your biggest fear?

_____

_____

21) Do you have any secrets?

_____

_____

22) Share a funny fact about yourself:

_____

_____

23) What is the best thing that has ever happened to you?

_____

_____

24) What is the worst thing that has ever happened to you?

_____

_____

25) What do you dream about?

_____

_____

AUTHOR NOTES ON THIS CHARACTER

Pretend you are alone with this character... who are they really?

_____

_____

What is special about them?

_____

_____

What is different about them?

_____

_____

Write 10 words about this character as if you have known them their whole life.

_____

_____

Draw or paste a picture of your character here:

CHARACTER TEN

1) What is your full name?

_____

2) How old are you and what is your gender or species?

_____

3) What colour is your hair; your eyes; your skin?

_____

4) Describe your physical appearance:

_____

_____

5) Who are your friends?

_____

_____

6) Who is your best friend?

_____

7) What do you like to do in your spare time?

_____

_____

8) Who are your parents?

_____

_____

9) Who are your grandparents?

_____

_____

10) Where do you live?

_____

_____

11) Where do you go to school?

_____

_____

12) Do you play sports? If so, what sports do you like to play?

_____

_____

13) Do you enjoy music? If so, what type of music do you like?

_____

_____

14) What are your likes?

_____

_____

15) What are your dislikes?

_____

_____

_____

16) Do you have any pets or are you a pet?

_____

_____

17) What makes you laugh?

_____

_____

18) What shocks or offends you?

_____

_____

19) What do you care about?

_____

_____

20) What is your biggest fear?

_____

_____

21) Do you have any secrets?

_____

_____

22) Share a funny fact about yourself:

_____

_____

23) What is the best thing that has ever happened to you?

_____

_____

24) What is the worst thing that has ever happened to you?

_____

_____

25) What do you dream about?

_____

_____

AUTHOR NOTES ON THIS CHARACTER

Pretend you are alone with this character... who are they really?

_____

_____

What is special about them?

_____

_____

What is different about them?

_____

_____

Write 10 words about this character as if you have known them their whole life.

_____

_____

Draw or paste a picture of your character here:

STORY PLANNING

You have two options here:

Option 1: Use the pages to actually write your story. There are 10 pages for each chapter, so you can easily write your story in this book to keep forever!

Or...

Option 2: Use the pages to pre-plan your story. Collect and write down your ideas over time. When you are finished planning your novel, open a word document on your computer and start writing your novel using all of the ideas that you have written in your Novel Assistant as your guide!

There are 2 pages devoted for "free writing." This is where you can write down any random ideas that pop into your head related to the story you are preparing to tell. This is a technique often used by authors to let their mind be free and creative! You never know what kind of ideas you can come up with, until you try this technique! Tip: get a notepad and do more free writing if it is helpful to you.

There are 2 pages for you to use story timelines and 2 pages for you to do your chapter planning. A story timeline is a way of planning out your story. Make a little horizontal line at the top of your timeline and write down what will happen first in your story. Then, make another line and write down what happens after that and so on until you fill up either one or both of your timelines with your story plot!

Properly planning out your story is a great way to stay focused on your writing! Now that you have your characters fully developed and have planned out your story ...you are ready to write!

Best of luck, writer!

NOVEL IDEAS:

FREE WRITING!!!

Write any ideas that pop into your head...anywhere on the page!

NOVEL IDEAS:

FREE WRITING!!!

Write any ideas that pop into your head...anywhere on the page!

TIMELINE

Create a Timeline by putting events in order here!

TIMELINE

Create a Timeline by putting events in order here!

CHAPTER PLANNING

Write one or two lines that sum up each chapter:

CHAPTER 1 -

CHAPTER 2 -

CHAPTER 3 -

CHAPTER 4 -

CHAPTER 5 -

CHAPTER 6 -

CHAPTER 7 -

CHAPTER 8 -

CHAPTER 9 -

CHAPTER 10 -

CHAPTER PLANNING

Write one or two lines that sum up each chapter:

CHAPTER 11 -

CHAPTER 12 -

CHAPTER 13 -

CHAPTER 14 -

CHAPTER 15 -

CHAPTER 16 -

CHAPTER 17 -

CHAPTER 18 -

CHAPTER 19 -

CHAPTER 20 –

Now that you have planned out your story…get ready to write!!!

CHAPTER ONE

Chapter Title

CHAPTER TWO

Chapter Title

CHAPTER THREE

Chapter Title

CHAPTER FOUR

Chapter Title

CHAPTER FIVE

Chapter Title

CHAPTER SIX

Chapter Title

CHAPTER SEVEN

Chapter Title

CHAPTER EIGHT

_____

Chapter Title

CHAPTER NINE

Chapter Title

CHAPTER TEN

_____

Chapter Title

CHAPTER ELEVEN

Chapter Title

CHAPTER TWELVE

Chapter Title

CHAPTER THIRTEEN

Chapter Title

CHAPTER FOURTEEN

Chapter Title

_____

_____

_____

_____

_____

_____

_____

_____

_____

_____

_____

_____

_____

_____

_____

_____

_____

_____

_____

_____

_____

_____

_____

CHAPTER FIFTEEN

Chapter Title

CHAPTER SIXTEEN

Chapter Title

CHAPTER SEVENTEEN

Chapter Title

CHAPTER EIGHTEEN

Chapter Title

CHAPTER NINETEEN

Chapter Title

CHAPTER TWENTY

Chapter Title

THE END!!!

Congratulations!!

Are you done? Of course you are, and we KNEW you could do it!!

Wondering what to do next? Well, celebrate...of course! You well deserve it! Writing a book is no easy task. Seeing it from start to finish is an awesome accomplishment and we would like to celebrate with you!

After you share your books with your parents, or your friends, or even your granny... Have them help you...

Send us a tweet at #NA4K on Twitter!

Share a photo of you and your finished book on our Facebook Page: NA4K

Or send us a message on our website at www.novelassistantpublishing.com

We would LOVE to hear from you!!

Then, go and write another book!!

NA4K!!

ABOUT NOVEL ASSISTANT

Novel Assistant was created by A.J. Mathews, an author who lives in a house over 150 years old in Ireland.

She lives in that old house with her husband, an Architectural Technologist, her 2 daughters, Laurel and Riley. They have 2 cats, Peter Pan and Lucy and a dog called Felix.

A.J. Mathews believes in all children and knows that if there is anyone who can write a story…it is

YOU!!!

CPSIA information can be obtained
at www.ICGtesting.com
Printed in the USA
LVHW010219151221
706268LV00014B/1871